All About Foxes

Denzel Carter

Rosen REAL READERS

Rosen Classroom™
New York

A fox is a small animal.

A baby fox is called a cub.

Foxes live in families.

Cubs are raised

by their parents.

Foxes live in the forest.
They have mostly brown
or red fur.

Foxes have thick fur.
This keeps them warm.

Arctic foxes live in
the North Pole.
They are white.

Foxes have large ears.
They have good hearing.

Foxes have a long snout.

They have a good sense of smell.

Foxes run fast.

They chase small animals.

Foxes eat small animals.
This fox eats a mouse.

Foxes also eat fruit and bugs.

This fox eats berries.

Words to Know

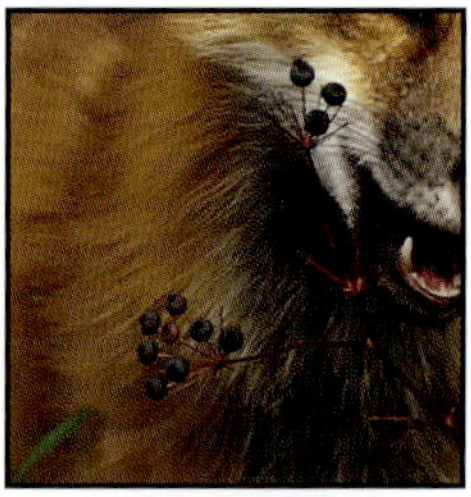

berries

ears

fox

fur